BOB CARLIN

Fiddle Tunes *for* Clawhammer Banjo

THANKS

to Doug and Bonnie Miller and Terri McMurray at whose homes
most of these tunes were written down, to Richard Carlin for
his editorial assistance, to Joel and Kathy Shimberg for
information on the tunes and to Henry Sapoznik, for his
help with the How to Read Tablature section.

A special thanks to Rounder Records for use of original
performances on the enclosed CD.

ISBN: 978-1-57424-250-8
SAN 683-8022

Cover photo by Matthew Spencer
BC-350+ Banjo photo courtesy of Gold Tone Inc. www.goldtone.com
Cover by James Creative Group

CENTERSTREAM

Biography

BOB CARLIN is international known as a master interpreter of the traditional style of banjo playing. In addition to four album for Rounder Records, he produced and performed on the ground breaking collection *Melodic Clawhammer Banjo* for Kicking Mu Records and produced several other banjo compendiums for that label. Bob has produced instructional DVDs for Homespun, M Bay and Goldtone, as well as writing a regular column for Banjo Newsletter. Additionally, Bob Carlin has his own line of "signa ture" banjos, the BC-120, BC-350 and BC-350+.

Bob Carlin with his Gold Tone BC- 350 banjo.
Photograph by Mathew Spencer.

Contents
& CD TRACK LIST

The Method Behind This Method

Welcome to the first book devoted totally to my own tablatures. This book is meant to complement my two Rounder CDs *Fiddle Tunes For Clawhammer Banjo* and *Where Did You Get That Hat?*. Although this contains the banjo arrangements found on those two records, the book can be used on its own.

This method is not meant to be an instruction manual on how to play clawhammer style banjo. Rather, it is a look at the way I approach traditional southern music and the five-string banjo through transcriptions of my playing. If you are looking for a tutor on the clawhammer style, may I suggest my beginner/intermediate DVD's published by Homespun and Goldtone.

A word on these tablatures: They are generalized transcriptions of my playing on the two Rounder albums since I never play a tune exactly the same way twice. Before the 1983 edition of this volume, long out-of-print, the majority of these tablatures have never been published.

"Box the Fox", "Dog on the Carport", "The Falls of Richmond", "Natural Bridge Blues", "Pays de Haut", "Say Darling Say", "Spotted Pony", "Sullivan's Hollow", and "Waiting for Nancy" all have guitar chords included in the tablatures. They are indicated by a chord letter above the tablature staff. I have included the guitar chords that are used on the record or, in the case of "Dog on the Carport" and "Waiting For Nancy", the back-up chords I play on the banjo. I leave it to the individual player to decide on the chords for the rest of the tunes. I think of many of these pieces melodically and rhythmically rather than chordally and would not use guitar back-ups.

The four digit number in the left hand corner of the tablatures, preceding the tune's title, indicates the album from which the arrangement comes. The number 0132 means *Fiddle Tunes For Clawhammer Banjo*, and 0172 means *Where Did You Get That Hat?*. The second number refers to the tune's placement on the album. As an example, the song "Ain't Gonna Get No Supper Here Tonight" has the numbers 0132, 2/4; it can be heard on the Fiddle Tunes album, on side two, track four. In the case where the letter a or b follows, the tune is part of a medley, "a" meaning the first tune, "b" meaning the second.

To the right of the tune title are five letters indicating the banjo tuning or banjo "key" used for the tune. They read fifth string to first string. In the case of the tunes utilizing fretted banjo, the capo position follows the tuning. With the fretless banjo, no capo can be used, and the notes represent the actual pitches of the strings.

The compact disc that is included in this book features excerpts of original recordings I made for Rounder Records back in 1979 and 1982. Published on the albums *Fiddle Tunes For Clawhammer Banjo* (Rounder 0132, 1980) and *Where Did You Get That Hat?* (Rounder 0172, 1982), the tablatures in this book and the performances from both recordings are placed in alphabetical order to facilitate your learning. They should help to give you a good idea of one time through each tune. In the case that I play an alternate version for one of the parts to a tune (such as the A part for "Box the Fox"), we've included that alternate version on the CD as well. In case you're interested in hearing whole performances, both albums are available through www.rounder archive.com as digital downloads or on physical CDs.

One last note: These arrangements are not the only way to play these tunes. Use them as a starting point in your own arrangements.

Good Luck!

4

How To Read Banjo Tablature

Tablature has been described as a musical "shorthand", in which the lines of the musical staff are each assigned a banjo string.

The lowest line signifies the fifth string, and the highest line signifies the first string.

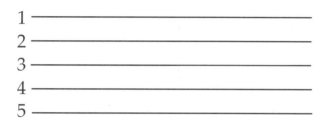

A number placed on a line show where to fret the string that line represents. Say you're in "double C" tuning (GCGCD). If the number 2 appears on the top staff line, you would play the first or D string at the second fret. If the number 3 appears on the third staff line from the top, fret the third string at the third fret. If the string is to be played open, a zero (0) is placed on the line corresponding to it.

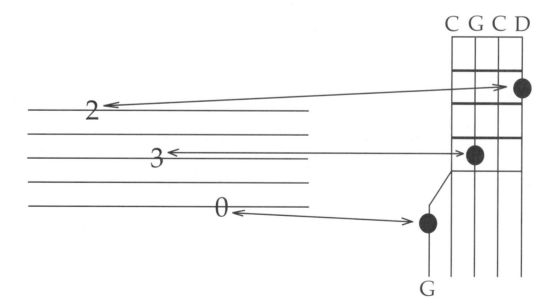

In the case of those tunes where a fretless banjo is used, fret numbers are approximate. In several cases, in-between fret numbers are used in an attempt to document what is being played (example: the fifth, sixth and seventh measures of the song "The Last Time").

Time Values

Each note in a tune has a time value, the most common being the quarter and the eighth notes.

The quarter note receives one beat (or foot stomp) whereas the eighth note reprersents half a beat (or half a quarter note). So in effect, two eighth notes have the same value as one quarter note.

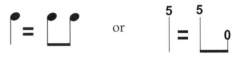

The quarter note in our tablature will always appear alone with a single stem coming down from it, while the eighths are usually in pairs with a connecting stem.

The quarters, incidently, are always played with the middle or index finger (some players use one, some the other, I use my index finger) while eighths can be gotten by either hammering, pulling off, sliding or using the thumb.

Thus, your typical strum would be notated as a quarter and two eighths:

or in tablature:

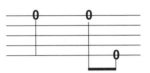

The letters under the staff tell how the strings are to be played to obtain the desired note:

Example

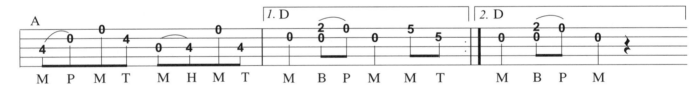

M-strike with the nail of the index or middle finger

T-pluck with the thumb

H-hammer on

P-pull off

SL-slide

B-brush

⎯⎯⎯ A "tie" is always placed above notes connected by a hammer on, pull off, or a slide.

The above outlines basic techniques used in each tune. Additional techniques are explained in the notes to each individual tune.

Ain't Gonna Get No Supper Here Tonight

TRACK 1

Source: Kenny Hall

0132-2/4

FCFCD-Capo 2

Pete Sutherland took this tune that Kenny Hall credits to Bob Wills' father John and changed it from the key of A to the key of G. The tune is in an F tuning that I use for the majority of fiddle tunes in the key of G (capoed at the second fret).

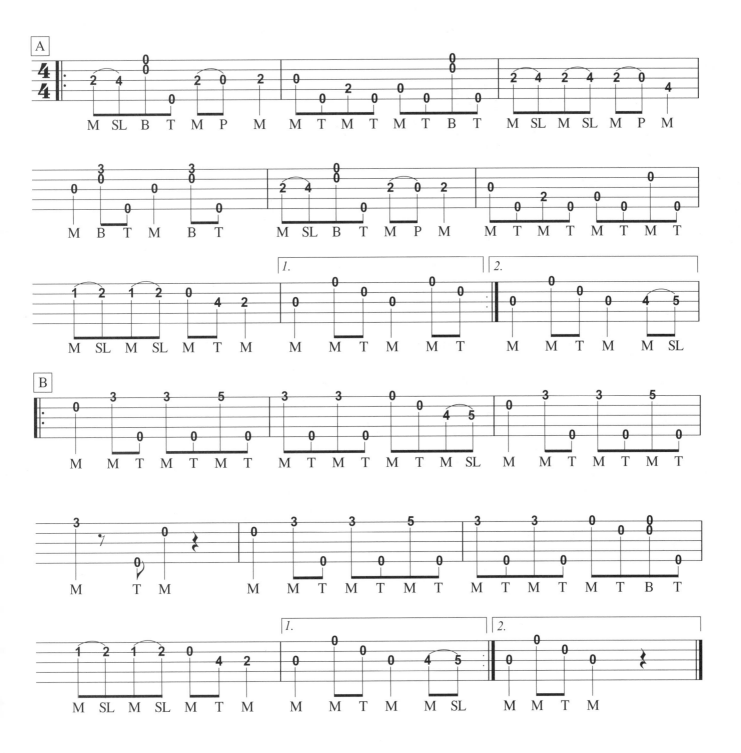

Bob buys a banjo from Shonan Hiratsuka, owner of Banjo Boy's Old Guitar Shop, Japan, 1995. Unidentified photographer.

Bob Carlin's Dream

TRACK 2

by Tony Trischka

0172-2/6a   FBbFCD

This tune revealed itself to Tony during the course of rehearsing for the album **Where Did You Get That Hat.**
It is played in a variation of the F tuning (FCFCD) with the fourth string dropped from C to Bb, changing the
tuning from the key of F to the key of Bb. I came up with this tuning, which I also use for "Tippy Get Your
Haircut", "Briar Picker Brown" and "Sugar Hill" (not included in this collection). In the fourth measure you
see the figure:

This is called an "open string pull off" and is accomplished by striking the third string with the middle or
index finger of your right hand and then pulling off an unstruck string. In this case, the second string is
pulled off with the index finger of your left hand.

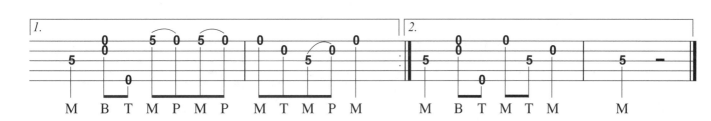

Briar Picker Brown

TRACK 3

Source: Buddy Thomas

0172-2/6b

FBbFCD

Buddy Thomas learned this tune which he played in the key of D from Morris Allen, a fiddler from Portsmouth, Ohio. Thomas, a fiddler from Kentucky, died in the mid- 1970s at the age of 39. Look at the figure found in the first and fifth measures of the (B) part:

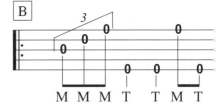

This is one of the variations on the "Galax lick". The triplet rhythm (see "Big Scioty") is mated with a slow brush across the third, second and first strings performed by the middle or index finger of the right hand.
Tuning: see "Bob Carlin's Dream"
Techniques: brush hammer on and held note – see "Big Scioty"
Recordings: "Kitty Puss", Buddy Thomas (Rounder Records)

Big Scioty

TRACK 4

Source: The Zenith String Band

0132-2/6   EBEBC#

A current hit on the old-time music charts, this is a tune from the playing of Burl Hammons of Marlington, West Virginia. His music is documented on **The Hammons Family** (Library of Congress) and **Shakin' Down the Acorns** (Rounder Records-Both now available in a single package from Rounder). "Big Scioty" is named for the Scioto River that flows through Ohio into the Ohio River. I have played with the Zenith String Band from Connecticut on occasion as a bass or banjo player. This tune is played in the same F tuning as "Ain't Gonna Get No Supper Tonight" tuned down one fret to the key of E.

In the first and third measures is the figure

This is just a normal hammer on occurring after a brush.

There is a similar figure in the second measure of the tune

The (B) part begins with a "triplet"

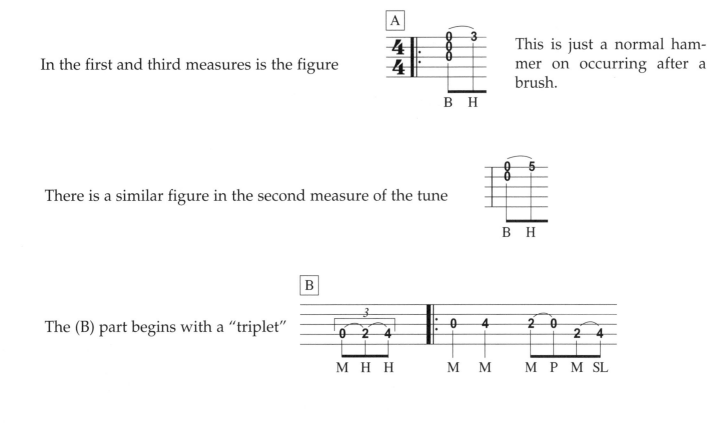

These three eighth notes are played as equal parts of the space filled normally by two eighth notes. This figure is repeated in the fourth measure and at the end of the first ending of the (B) part. At the end of the second measure/beginning of the third measure of the same part is a "held note"

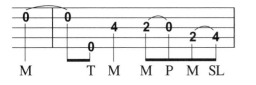

The first note is struck with the middle or index finger of the right hand and is allowed to ring over into the first beat of the third measure.

Recordings: **Ship In The Clouds**, Andy Cahan, Laura Fishleder and Lisa Ornstein (Folkways Records); **Pigtown Fling**, (Green Linnet Records); **Wheatland Festival 1978**, the Henrie Brothers (Wheatland Records); **Shaking Down The Acorns**, Burl Hammons (Rounder Records)

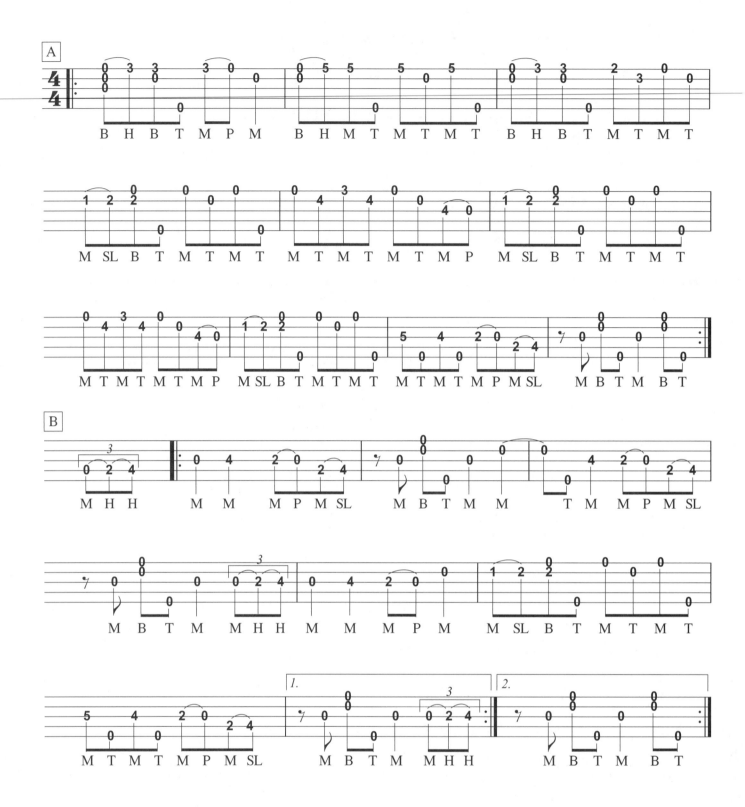

Box the Fox

 TRACK 5

Source: Bruce Hutton

0132-1/7a   GCGCD-Capo 2

Some melodic clawhammer banjo for those fans of the album of the same name. Washingtonian Bruce Hutton, a member of the Double Decker String Band, taught me this tune. It is originally from Pennsylvania. The (A) part ends with a figure similar to the brush hammer used in "Big Scioty". It is a "brush pull off" and works the same way as a normal pull off, occurring after the brush. In the forth measure of the (B) part, there is a "dotted eighth note".

A dot after a note adds half the value of the note onto itself. In this case, hold the note the length of an eighth and a sixteenth note added together:

Techniques: open string pull off – see "Bob Carlin's Dream"

Recordings: Old Time Music–It's All Around, Bruce Hutton (Folkways Records); Second Annual **Brandywine Mountain Music Convention,** Tracy Schwartz and Mike Seeger (Heritage Records)

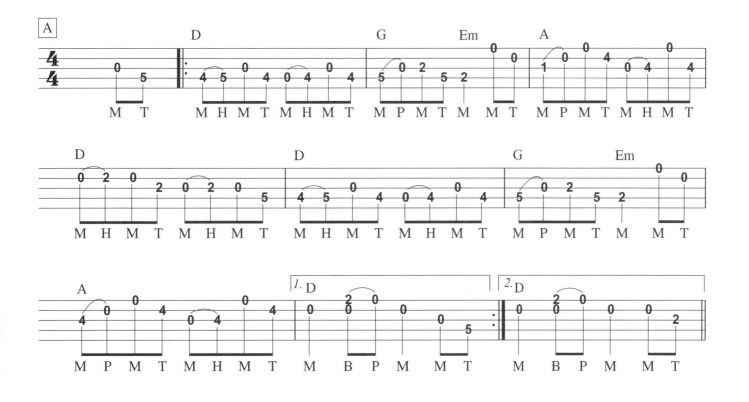

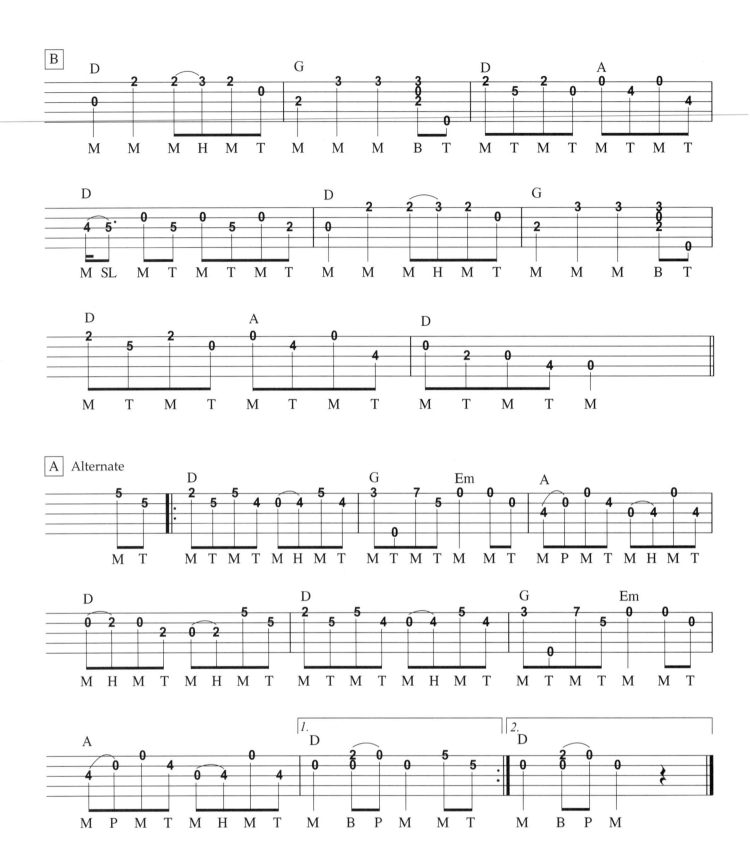

14

Chilly Winds

TRACK 6

Source: Lee Pulver Buildings and the Single Bounds

0132-2/7   EEoctave EG#B

The early 1970s was a boom time for the old-time music scene around New York City. Weekly sessions were held at the Galaway Bay Tavern. We were all learning from each other. At the same time, Ray Alden, who introduced most of us to the music of Tommy Jarrell and Fred Cockerham, held regular get-togethers and rehearsals for a loose band called alternately "Ben Steele and His Bare Hands", "Root, Hog, or Die" and "Lee Pulver". I played guitar for the band, which also included Dave Spilkia, Hank Sapoznik, Colin Quigely and Woody Woodring. "Chilly Winds" is played in a tuning used by Tommy Jarrell for the tune "John Brown's Dream". It is normal G tuning (GDGBD), with the fourth string dropped to an octave below the third string. I tune the banjo down three frets to the key of E.

Recordings: **"Music From Round Peak"** (Heritage Records)

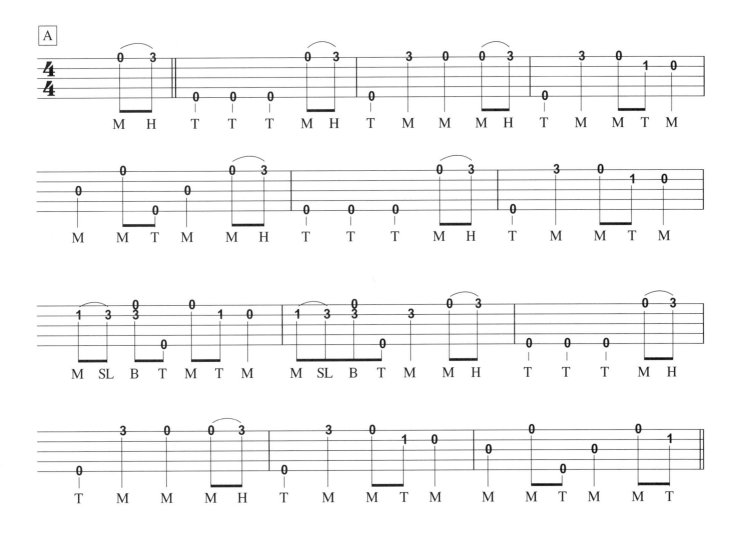

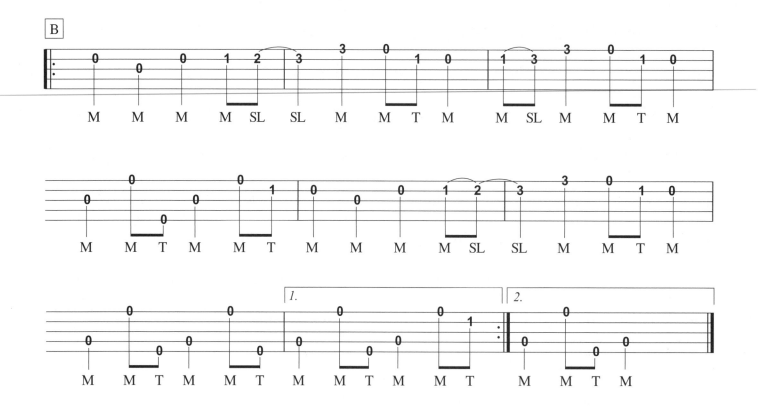

I'm a going where those chilly winds, those chilly winds don't blow
I'm a going where those chilly winds don't blow
Repeat 1st line
Going to my long lonesome, long lonesome home
Headed for my long lonesome home.

I'm a going where the weather suits, the weather suits my clothes
I'm a going where the weather suits my clothes
Repeat 1st line
Going to my long lonesome, long lonesome home
Headed for my long lonesome home.

I'm going where the water tastes, the water tastes like wine
I'm going where the water tastes like wine
Repeat 1st line
Going to my long lonesome, long lonesome home
Headed for my long lonesome home.

Oh when I'm gone don't you weep, don't you weep for me
Oh when I'm gone don't you weep for me
Repeat 1st line
Cause I'm going to my long lonesome, long lonesome home
Headed for my long lonesome home

Repeat the 1st verse

Clinch Mountain Backstep

TRACK 7

Source: Tracy Schwartz

0132-1/5 GDGBD-Capo 2

Pete Sutherland learned this version of Ralph Stanley's bluegrass banjo tune from Tracy Schwartz at a recording session for **Potluck and Dance Tonight**. Tracy calls his version "Liza Jane".

Techniques: Galax lick: brush-see "Briar Picker Brown"
Recordings: **Potluck and Dance Tonight**, Sandy Bradley with Tracy Schwartz (Fretless/Alacazar Records);
Stanley Brothers and the Clinch Mountain Boys (King/Gusto Records)

by Ralph Stanley

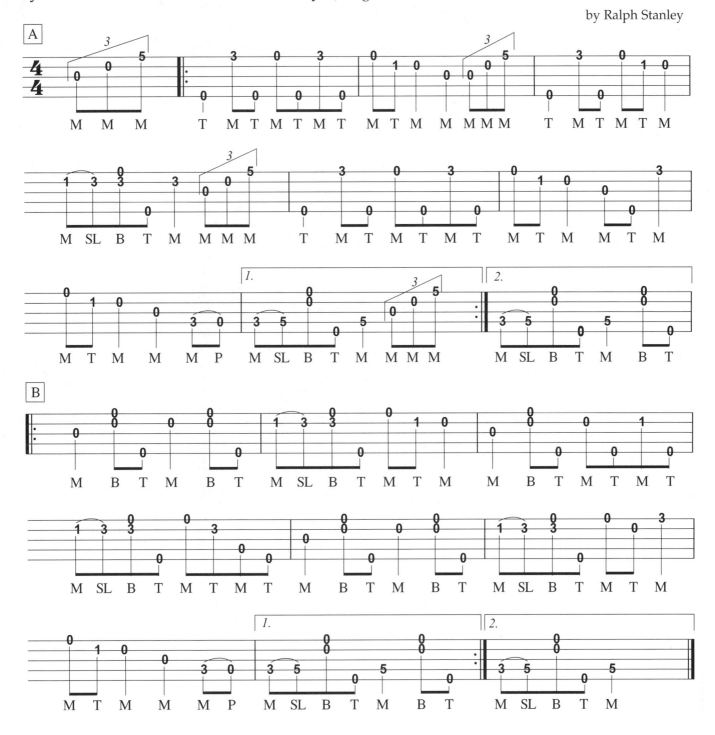

Bob Carlin, as a member of the Hartford String Band, backs up John Hartford's fiddling on the main stage at Merlefest 2000. Photograph by Frank Serio.

Davy Davy

TRACK 8

Source: Judy Hyman and Jeff Claus

0132-2/5   GCGCD-Capo 2

This is a version of "Going Down The River". Jeff and Judy, now residing outside of Ithaca, New York, are two of my favorite musicians on guitar and fiddle, respectively. A C chord (capoed up two frets becoming a D chord) is used in the first three measures of this tune. The second string is fretted with the index finger and the first string is fretted with the ring finger of the left hand.

This tune uses a variation of the Galax lick explained in the notes to "Briar Picker Brown" the "Galax lick: brush". For example, in the sixth measure of the (B) part is the figure:

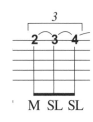

This is just a slide in triplet rhythm instead of the roll used in "Briar Picker Brown". It continues into the next measure, with the sliding finger of the left hand reaching the fifth fret of the first string at the same time that the fifth string is sounded with the thumb of the right hand.

Techniques: Dotted eighth note-see "Box the Fox"

Recordings: Echoes of the Ozarks Volume Three, Weems String Band (County Records)

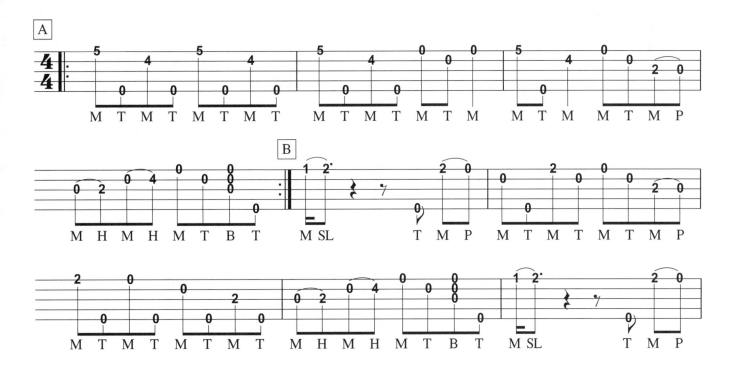

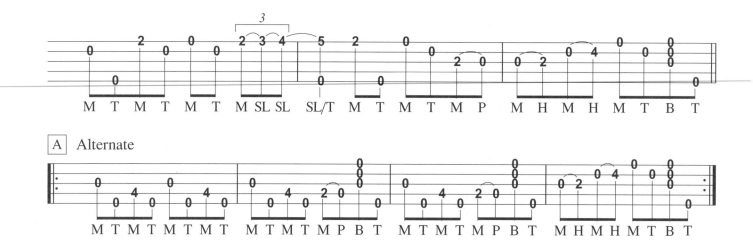

A | Alternate

Bob Carlin (on ground) with the Horseflies at the 1988 Philadelphia Folk Festival, Jeff Claus is second from the left and Judy Hyman is with fiddle fourth from the left. Photograph by Armen Kachaturian.

Dog On The Carport

TRACK 9

Source: Ruth Dornfeld

GDGBD-Capo 2

As mentioned in the introduction to this book , the guitar chords in the second part of this tune refer to chord positions used by the banjo. Therefore, you should be holding down a C chord position (capoed up to a D chord) in the (B) part, second measure:

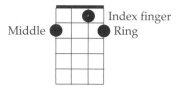

An F chord position (capoed up to G) in the third measure:

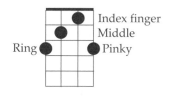

And a Bb chord position (capoed up to C) in the fourth measure:

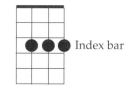

Techniques: Galax lick: slide-see "Davy Davy"

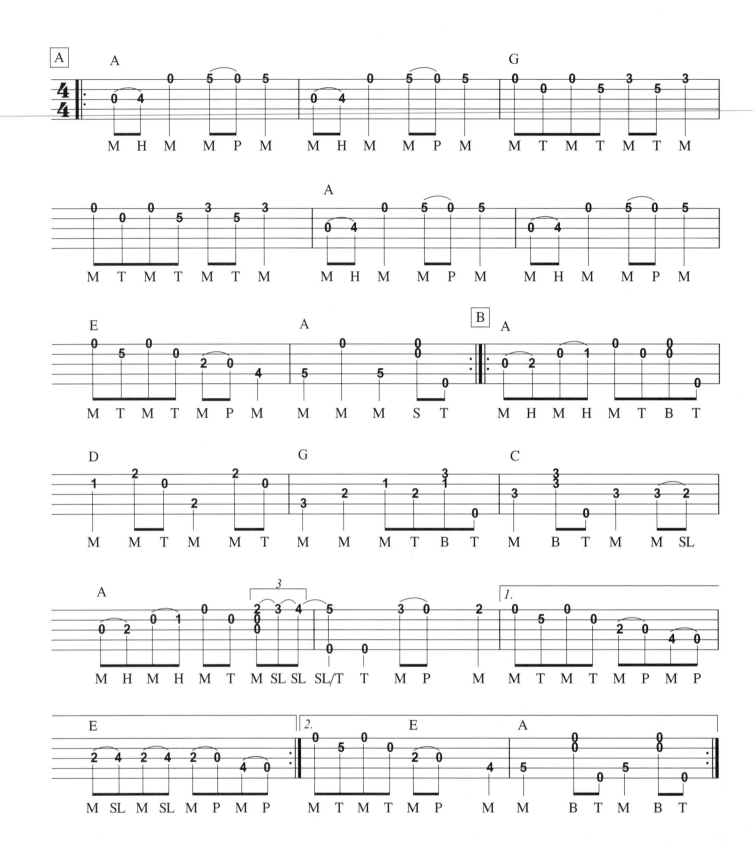

"A Tribute to John Hartford" presented by the public radio program Mountain Stage at the War Memorial Auditorium, Nashville, TN, September 24, 2000. This concert featured an "All-star" cast, including Bob as a member of the Hartford String Band. Pictured here is the finale featuring (left to right): unidentified camera man, John Cowan (clapping), John Hartford, Norman Blake/guitar, David Rawlings/guitar, Gillian Welch (blocked by Bob), Bob Carlin/banjo, Mike Compton/mandolin (at microphone), Ron Sowell/guitar (with headphones, from the Mountain Stage Band), Bela Fleck/banjo, Chris Sharp/guitar (at microphone) and Larry Perkins/bass. Photographer unknown.

The Falls of Richmond

TRACK 10

Source: **Summer Oaks and Porch,**
The Fuzzy Mountain String Band (Rounder Records)

0132-2/2   GDGCD-Capo 2

This album was a prime influence on me when I started playing old-time music. The triplet used in the second measure is a double pull-off in the triplet rhythm.

Techniques: Dotted eighth note-see "Box the Fox"; Galax lick: brush-see "Briar Picker Brown"

Bob Carlin giving a banjo workshop at the 2007 Philadelphia Folk Festival.
Photograph by C. Ernest Tedino.

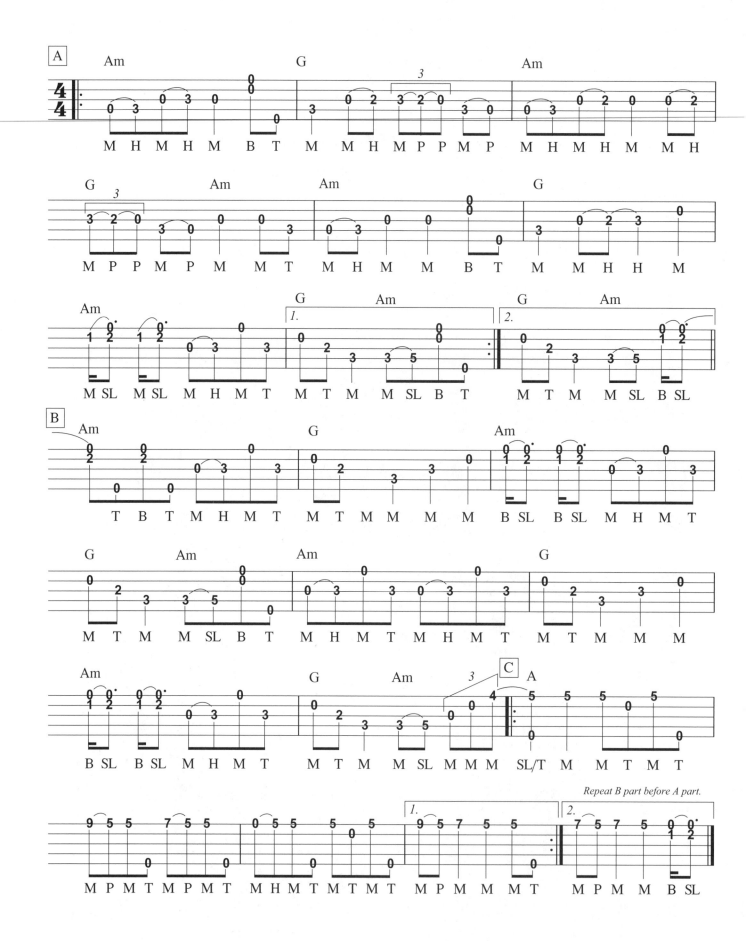

Garfield

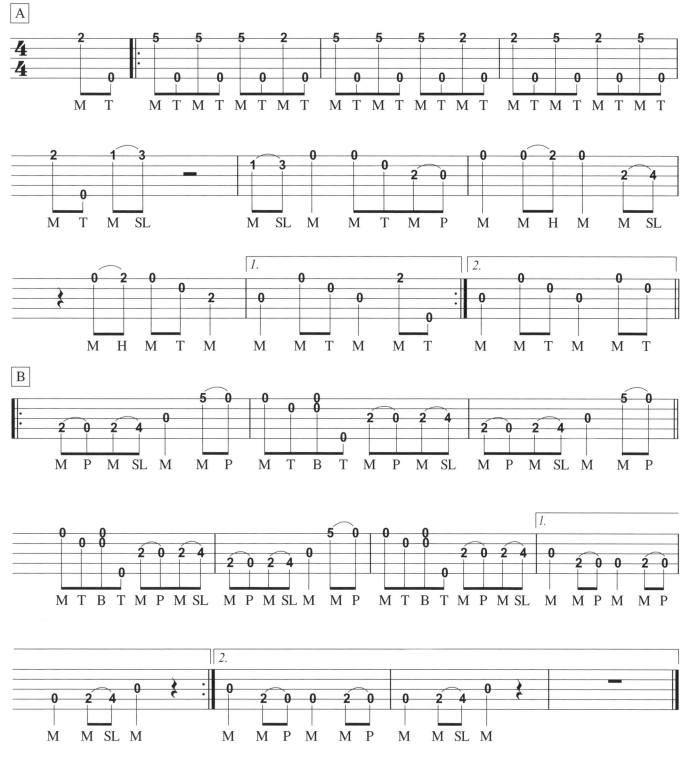

TRACK 11

Source: Stanley Bailey

0172-2/3

AEAC#E Fretless

Mr. Bailey is a sixty-seven year old fiddling hog farmer residing in Southern Georgia. He comes from a musical family and learned to play at age eight from his older brother and his uncle Tom Dixon. Dixon, from
Thomasville, was married to Bailey's father's sister. He played this tune in the "cross-tuned" key of A.

Recordings: Bluejeans and Lace (with Stanley Bailey) (Eagle Records)

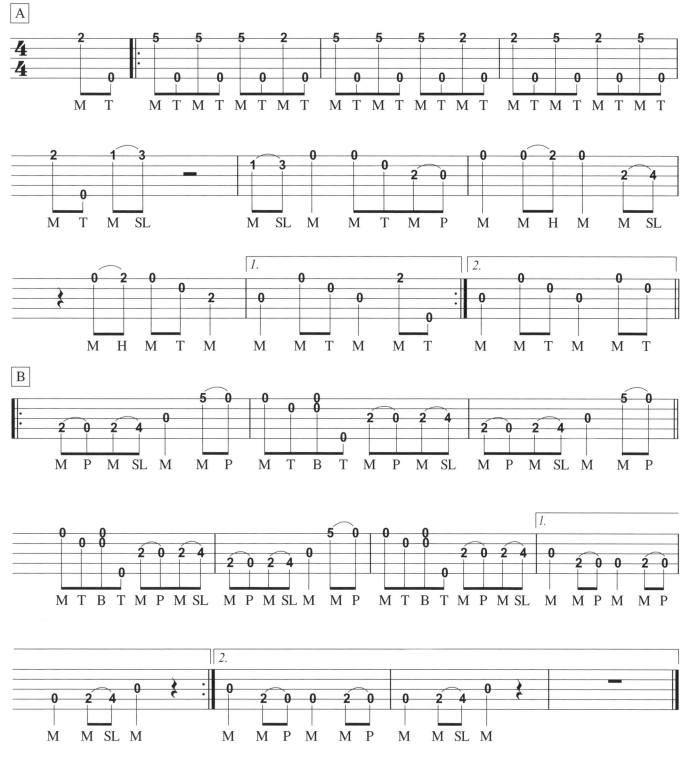

Icy Mountain

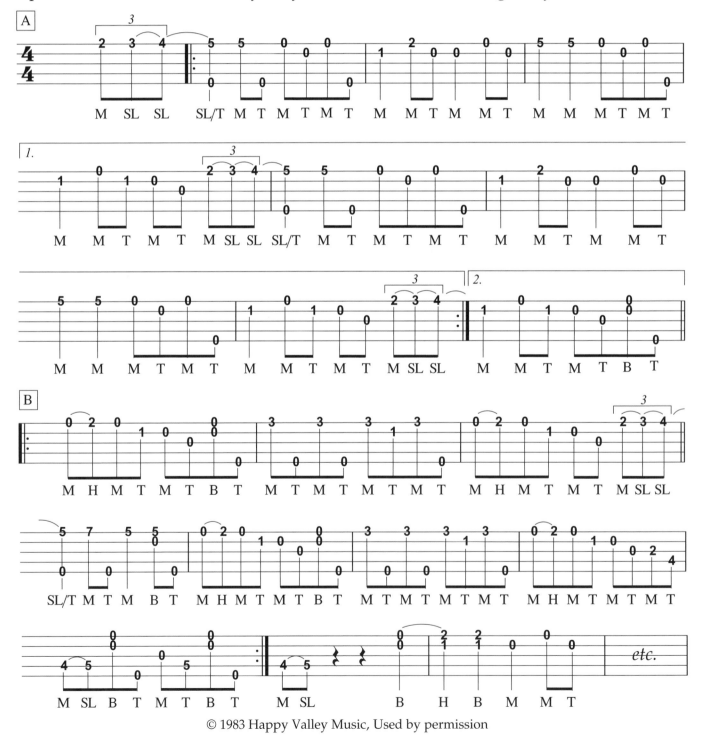

TRACK 12

Source: Ward Jarvis

0132-2/1   GDGBD-Capo 2

"That Icy Mountain?" " I learnt that there from a fellow by the name of Sandy, a good fiddler, lived in Clay
County way years ago." "What was his first name?" "Frank, Frank Sandy. Left-handed fiddler", —from a
conversation between Ward Jarvis and Carl Fleischhauer. Ward Jarvis (1894-1982) was a fiddler and banjo
player from Braxton County, West Virginia. He moved to Southeastern Ohio in 1947. Dana Loomis, a school-
mate of my brother Richard, brought my brother to visit Ward. Richard supplied me with a copy of the tapes
they made, from which I learned "Icy Mountain" and many other tunes unique to Ward. The "dropped beat"
was conceived by Pete Sutherland.

Techniques: Galax lick: slide-see "Davy Davy"; Brush Hammer on-see "Big Scioty"

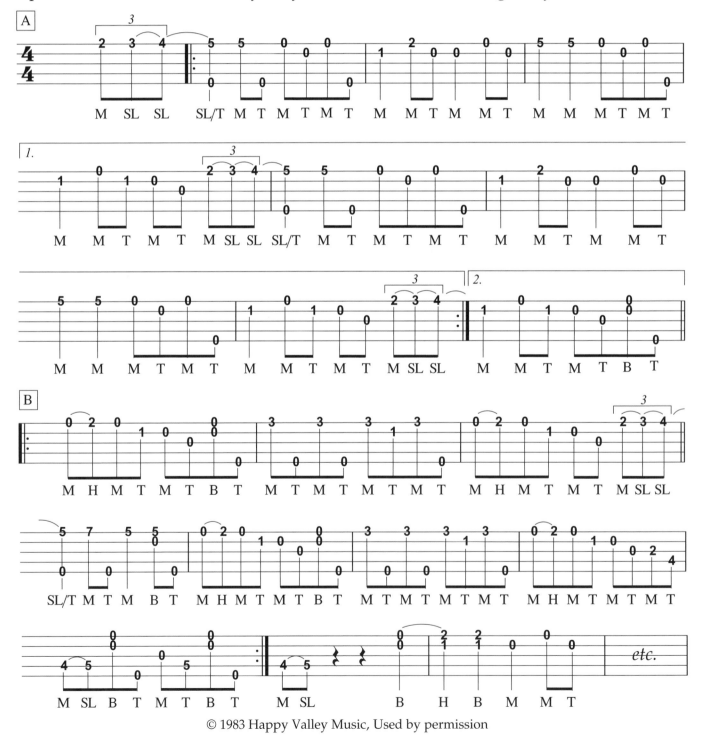

26

Indiana Breakdown

TRACK 13

0172-1/4

AEAC#E Fretless

Techniques: held note-see "Big Scioty"; Galax lick: slide-see "Davy Davy"

by Pete Sutherland

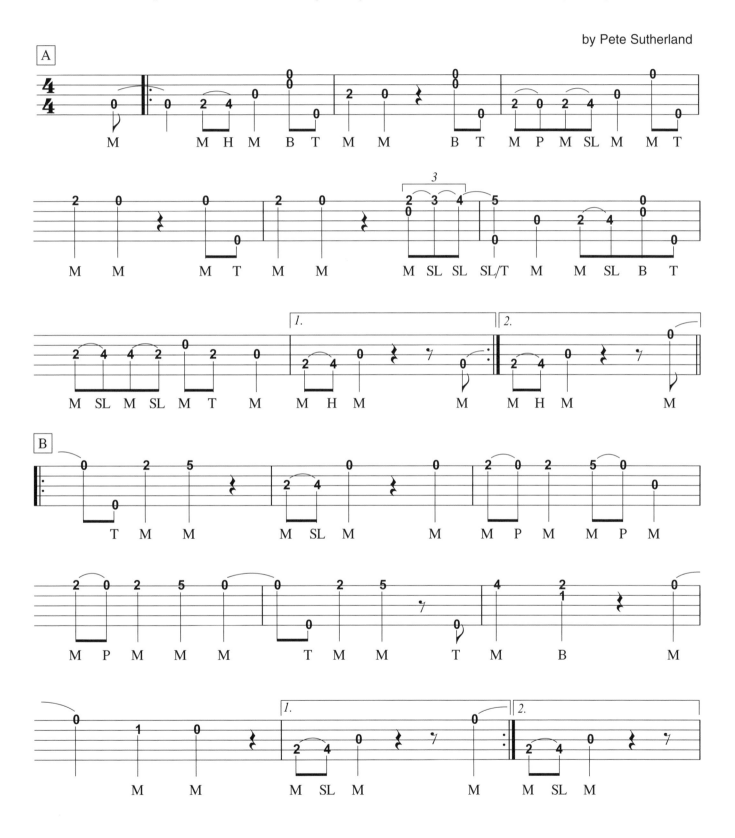

Ladies On The Steamboat

TRACK 14

Source: **A Ramblin' Reckless Hobo,**
Burnett and Rutherford (Rounder Records)

0172-1/1   FCFCD-Fretless

Dick Burnett was a blind banjo player, fiddler, and singer who, at the age of twenty-four, lost his sight in an attack by a robber. Leonard Rutherford was his fiddling partner and was seventeen years his junior. From Wayne County, Kentucky, they were musical partners for thirty-five years. In 1927, Burnett and Rutherford recorded this tune for Columbia Records that they probably learnt from fiddler Ed Haley. This tune is normally played in the key of G.

Tuning: F (see "Ain't Gonna Get No Supper Here Tonight")
Recordings: Monticello, Gregory and Davenport (Davis Unlimited Records).

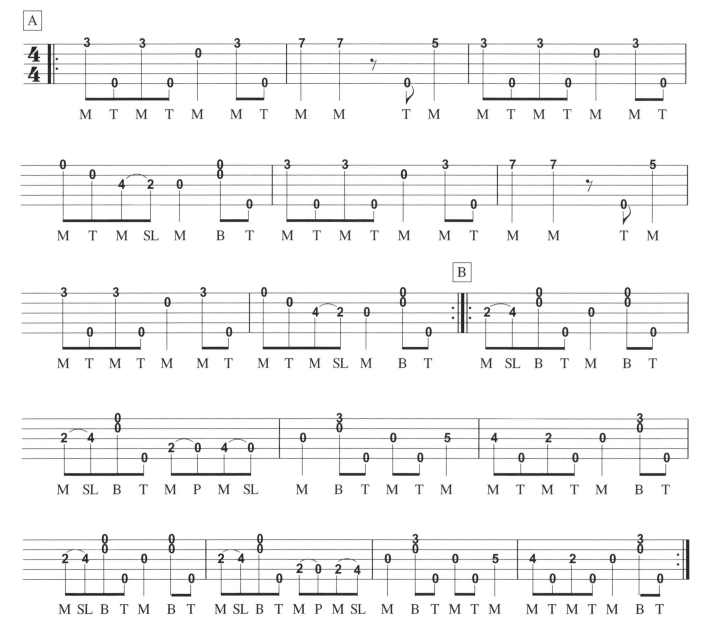

28

The Last Time

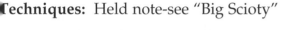 TRACK 15

Source: **Out of Our Heads,** The Rolling Stones (London Records)

0172-2/2 FCFCD-Fretless

This arrangement started in an offhand way. Its success pushed me to experiment with setting other rock'n'roll tunes on the banjo. Since that time, I have arranged other tunes by the Rolling Stones and the Beatles.

Tuning: F (see "Ain't Gonna Get No Supper Here Tonight")
Techniques: Held note-see "Big Scioty"

Bob Carlin, Merlefest, 2000, in front of John Hartford's bus.
Photograph by Mac Carbonell.

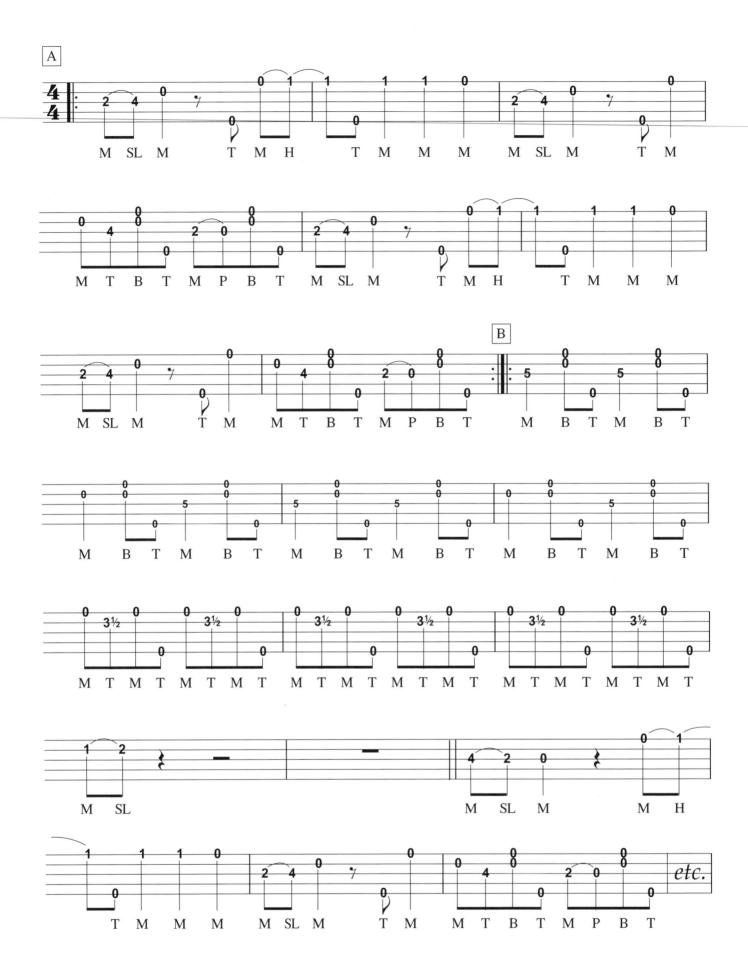

Natural Bridge Blues

TRACK 16

Source: Fred Cockerham

0172-2/4

GDGBD-Fretless

I met Fred Cockerham in the mid-1970s at several concerts in and around the New York City area. We continued to be friends until his death several years ago. Fred's fretless banjo playing has been a prime source of inspiration for my playing of that instrument. Tommy Magness (1911-1972) fiddled with Roy Acuff, Arthur Smith and Bill Monroe, among others. In 1941, he was a member of Roy Hall's Blue Ridge Entertainers with whom he first recorded this tune.

Recordings: Roy Hall and His Blue Ridge Entertainers (County Records)

by Tommy Magness

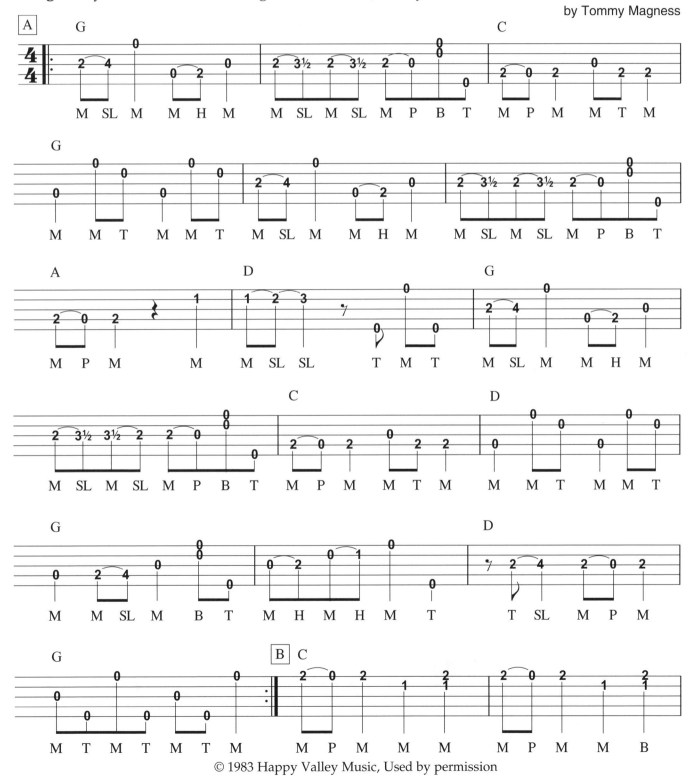

31

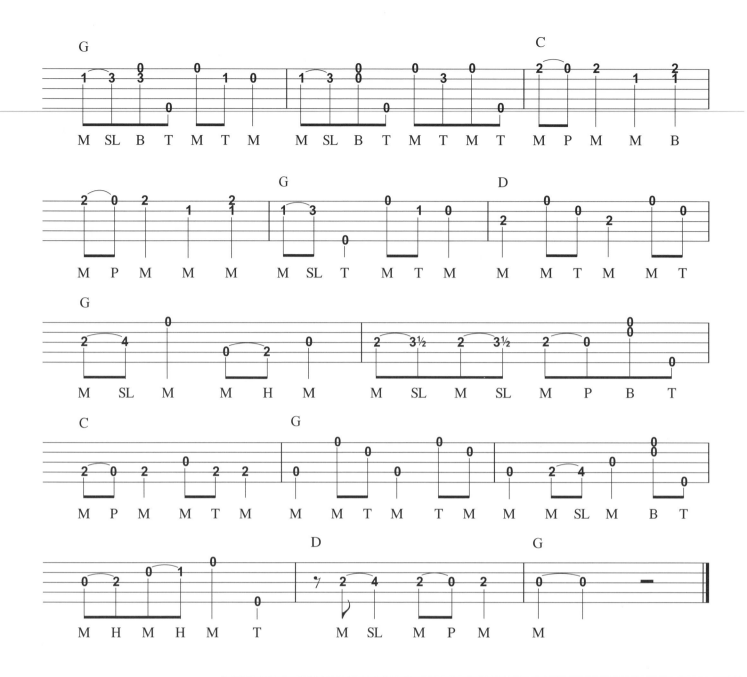

Oh the natural bridge it's calling me,
I don't know what to do
Here I am, left me here, stranded
with the blues.

Oh my God, Oh my Lord, I don't
know what to do
Natural Bridge is calling me and I
don't know where to go.

Fred Cockerham on the left with Bob Carlin outside of Fred's North Carolina home, circa 1978. Photographer unknown.

Needlecase

TRACK 17

Source: Al Lubanes

0132-1/1

GCGCD-Capo 2

It was Al Lubanes' rendition of this tune on the fiddle (backed by banjo and conga drum!) at the Trumansburg Fiddle Contest that inspired me to really learn it. Sam McGee is responsible for putting "Needlecase" into current circulation through his finger-picked banjo recording.

Techniques: Galaz lick: brush –see "Briar Picker Brown", brush hammer- see "Big Scioty"
Recording: The McGee Bros and Arthur Smith (Folkways Records)

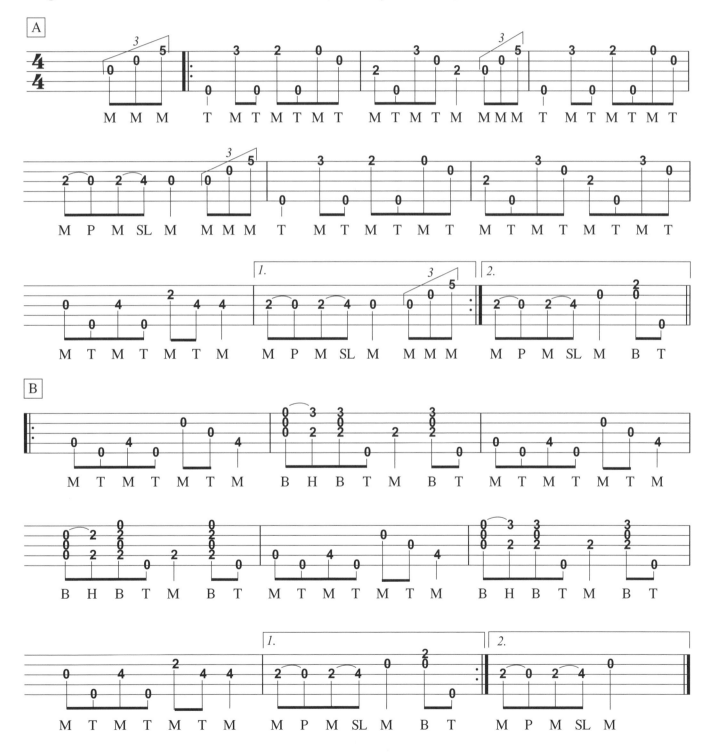

Pays de Haut

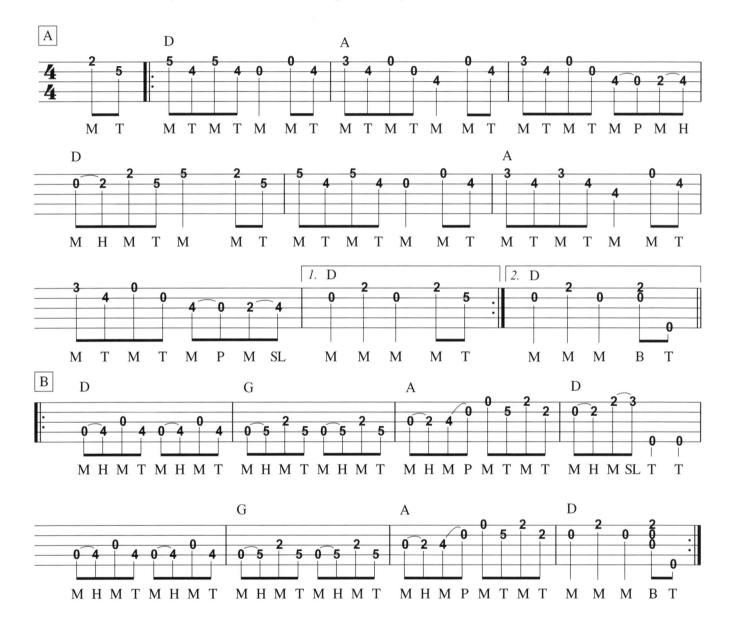

TRACK 18

Source: Applejack

0132-1/7b

GCGCD-Capo 2

I learned this tune while sitting in the contra dance band Applejack at a Chelsea House dance in Vermont. It is French-Canadian in origin and translates as "high country".

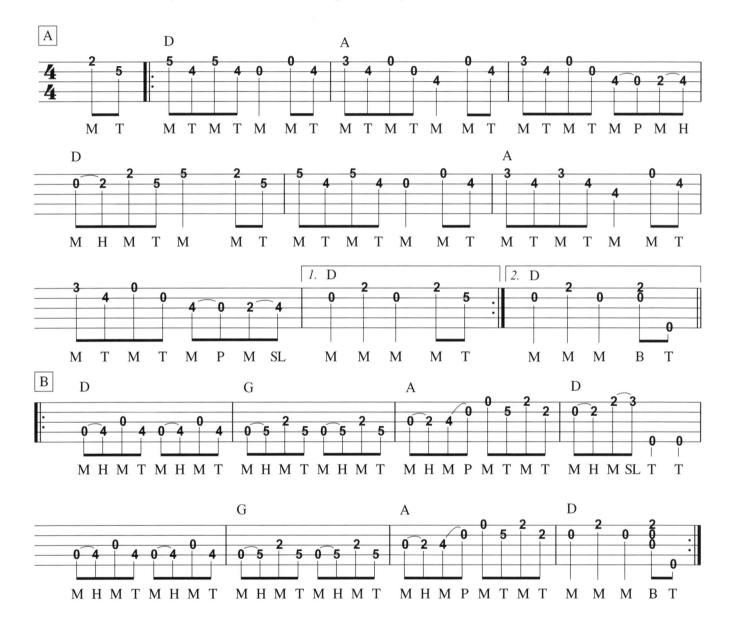

Payday

TRACK 19

Source: John Hurt

0172-1/5

F#ADAD-Fretless

My early contact with traditional music was through the recordings of country blues guitarists such as Gary Davis, Blind Blake and John Hurt. Hurt, from Avalon, Mississippi, had a brief recording career for Okeh Records in 1928. He was rediscovered in 1963 and performed for urban audiences until his death in 1967.

Tuning: "Dead Man's tuning"
Techniques: Held note – see "Big Scioty"
Recordings: Mississippi John Hurt Today (Vanguard Records); **Shuffle Rag**, Andy Cohen (June Appal Records)

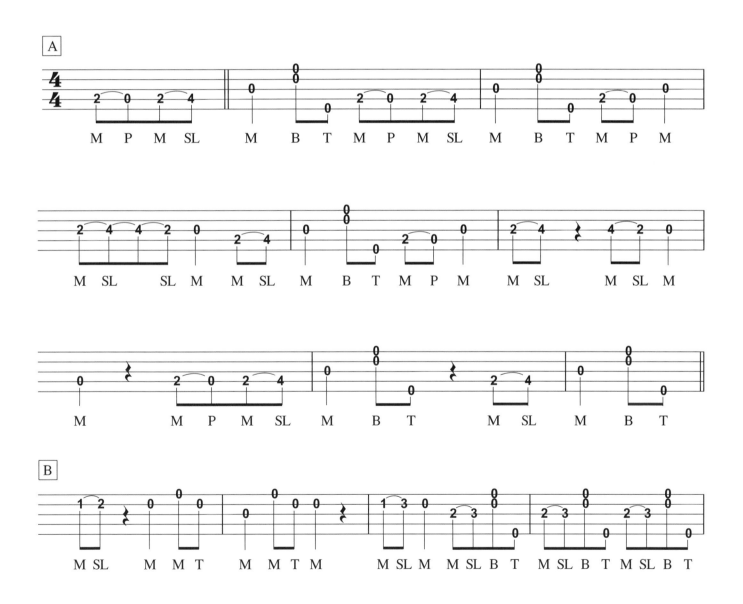

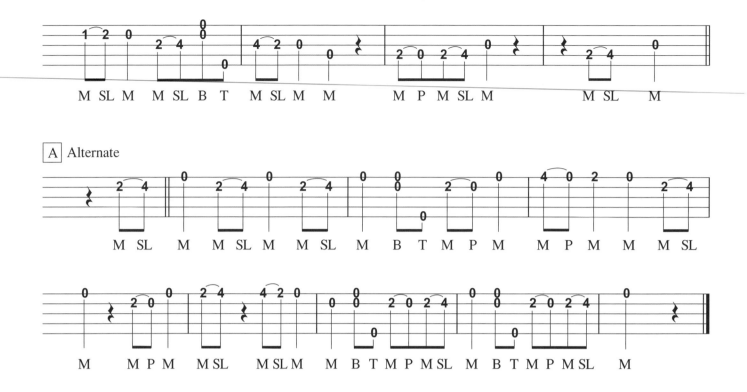

You can walk, you better run, you better…your fun
I'm gonna give it to you mama, next payday
Payday, Payday
I'm gonna give it to you mama, next payday.

For there's a rabbit in the log
I ain't got my rabbit dog
And I hate to let that rabbit get away
Get away, get away
Lord, I hate to let that rabbit get away.

For I've done everything I could do
Just to try and get along with you
I'm gonna take you to your mama, next payday
Payday, Payday
I'm gonna take you to your mama next payday.

Repeat 1st verse.

Pretty Little Indian

TRACK 20

Source: The Hotmud Family

0132-1/6   GDGCD-Capo 2

A fiddle tune from Southern Ohio, an area rich in old-time and bluegrass music. The tune comes from Van Kidwell, a fiddler from Kentucky now living in Ohio. Musicians like Van, who migrated from West Virginia and Kentucky, influenced Ohio's music greatly.

Techniques: Open string pull off see-"Bob Carlin's Dream"
Recordings: Fiddlin' Van Kidwell with the Hotmud Family (Vetco Records)

Photograph by David Weatherly.

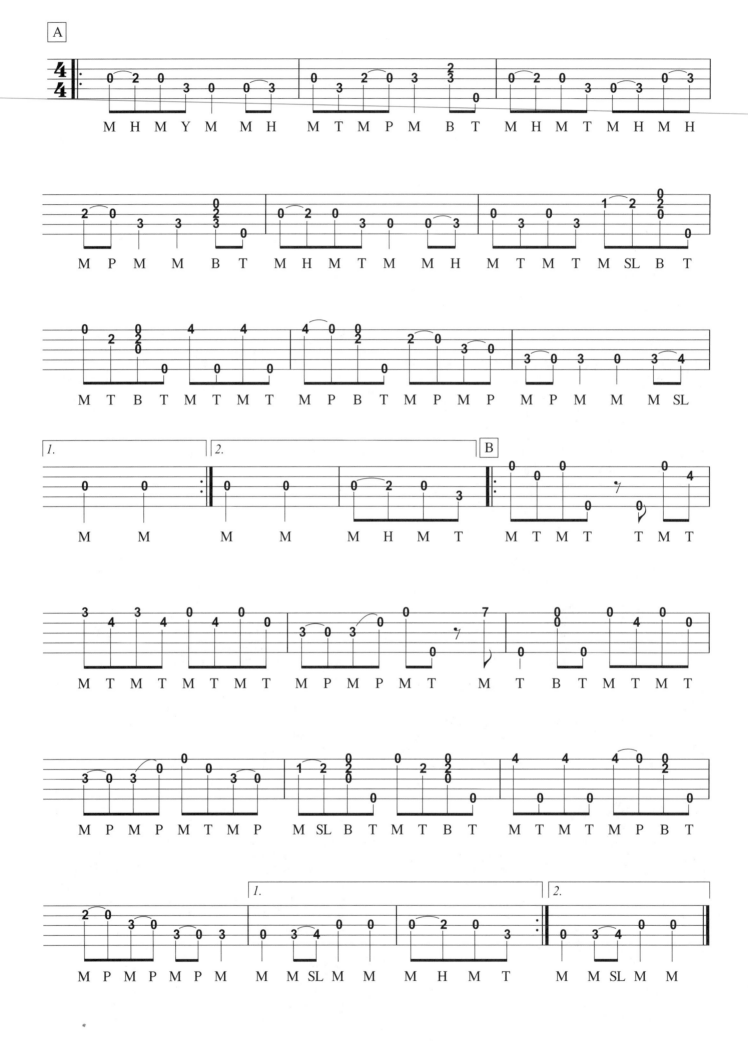

Rat Cheer

TRACK 21

GCGCD-Capo 2

This tune was written for the fiddle by Pete Sutherland who plays on both of my Rounder albums. He performs with Grey Larson and Malcolm Dalglish in an ensemble that highlights original tunes and songs.

Techniques: Galax lick: slide –see "Davy Davy"; held note-see "Big Scioty"; brush pull off –see "Box the Fox"

by Pete Sutherland

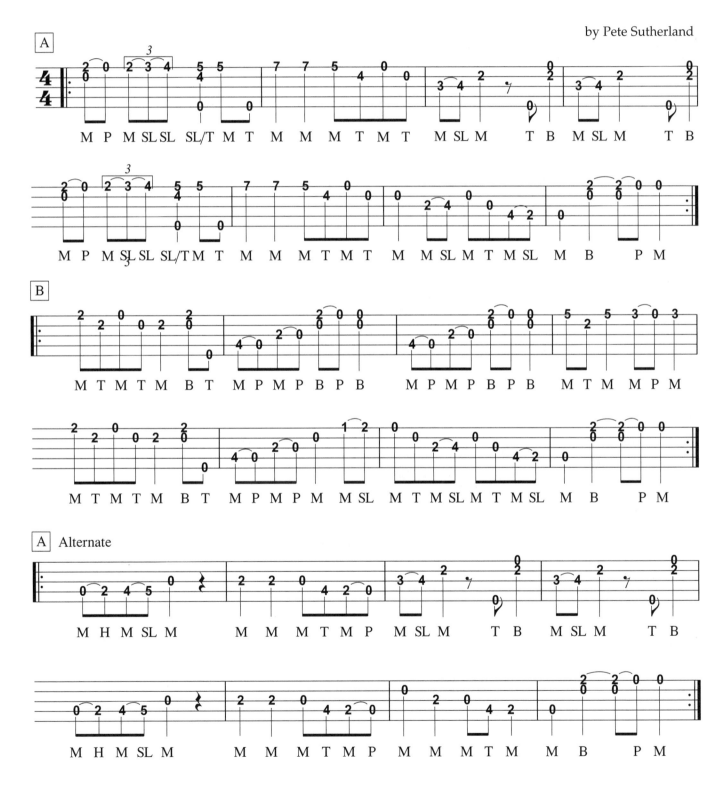

Rye Straw

TRACK 22

Source: Tommy Jarrell

0132-1/2b

GCGCD-Capo 2

Called "The Joke on the Puppy" by Tommy, "Rye Straw" is my arrangement of his fiddle version on the banjo. The tune dates back to at least the 1880's, when it was published under the title "A Whoop From Arkansas" by George Cole of Boston.

Techniques: Galax lick: brush-see "Briar Picker Brown"; Galax lick: slide-see "Davy Davy"; brush pull off-see "Box the Fox".

Recordings: Sail Away Ladies, Tommy Jarrell (solo fiddle) (County Records); **Joke on the Puppy**, Tommy Jarrell (with band) (Mountain Records)

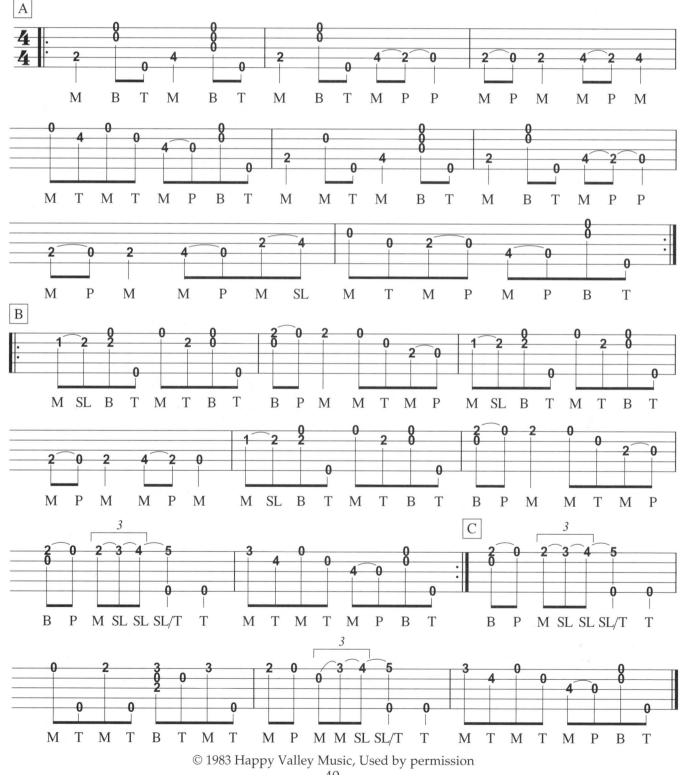

Sadie At The Backdoor

0172-1/3   GCGCD-Capo 2

This tune was written to document what Sadie, Jere's cat, sounded like meowing at the backdoor immediately after being let out of the front. Jere taught it on banjo to his fiddling brother Greg, from who I learnt the tune.

Techniques: Galax lick: brush-see "Briar Picker Brown"; brush pull off and dotted eighth note –see :"Box the Fox"; held note –see "Big Scioty".

Recordings: Foolish Questions, Sandy Bradley and the Small Wonder String Band (Rooster Records).

by Jere Canote

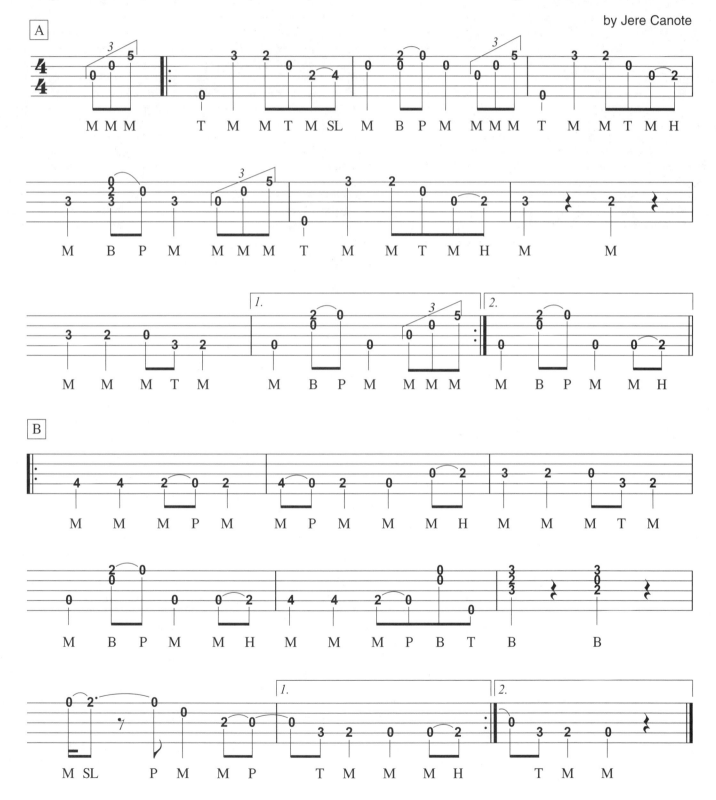

Jere Canote (on left) and Bob Carlin try out one of Jere's minstrel banjos at the Festival of American Fiddle Tunes, Port Townsend, Washington. Photograhper unknown.

Say Darling Say

Source: Bruce Molsky

0172-2/7   FBbFBbC

Bruce, a fiddler, banjo player and guitarist now residing in Washington, D.C., is an acquaintance from the mid- 1970s when I was based in New York City. He has been a constant source of tunes and musical inspiration. Bruce learned this song from Paul Brown, who learned it from Fields Ward. It is played here in double C tuning (GCGCD) tuned down two frets to the key of Bb.

Techniques: brush hammer on – see "Big Scioty"; brush pull off –see "Box the Fox"; Galax lick: slide – see "Davy Davy".

Recordings: Round the Heart of Old Galax-Volume Three, E.V. Stoneman (County Records)

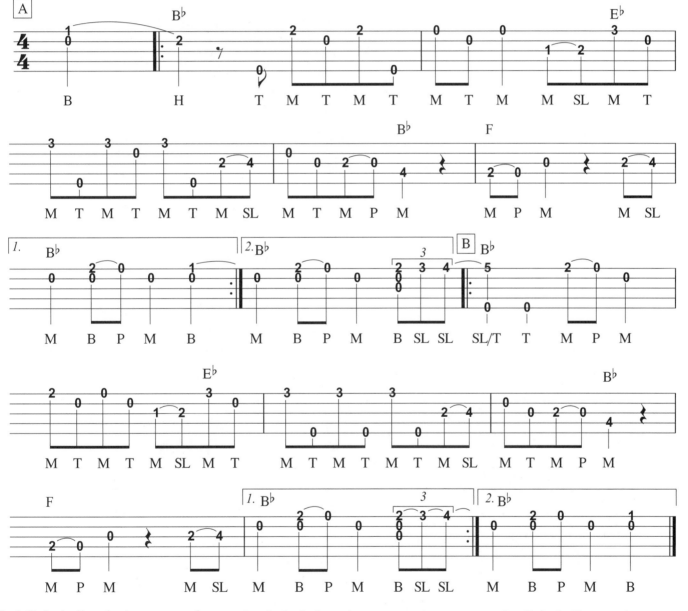

Hush little darling don't say a word,
I'm gonna buy you a mockingbird.
Say Darling Say
If that mockingbird won't sing,
I'm gonna buy you a diamond ring.
Say Darling Say

Say little darling if you were mine
Wouldn't do nothing buy starch and iron.
Say Darling Say
Starch and iron would be your trade
I'd get drunk and lay in the shade.
Say Darling Say

Say little darling won't you marry me
We'll build a house by the old oak tree.
Say Darling Say
We'll build a house by the old oak tree
Two little babies sitting on my knee.

Bruce Molsky (standing with Fiddle) and Bob Carlin (sitting with banjo) Circa 1988
Photograph by Carl Fleischhauer.

Shady Grove

TRACK 25

Source: **Old Originals Volume One,** Sam Connor (Rounder Records)

0132-1/3

GDGCD-Capo 2

This version is called "Salt River" by fiddler Sam Connor on Tom Carter and Blanton Owen's excellent collection of music from Southwestern Virginia.

The Spotted Pony

TRACK 26

Source: Cindy Swiatlowski

0132-1/4a

GCGCD-Capo 2

Cindy, a banjoist and dancer residing in Charlottesville, Virginia, taught me "The Spotted Pony" the firs
time we met at "Breaking Up Christmas". "Christmas" was an annual three day New Year's party held in
Lexington, Virginia that provided the opportunity for old-time musicians and dancers from the east coast to
meet and play together.

Recordings: Sycamore Tea, Dutch Cove Old Time String Band (June Appal Records)

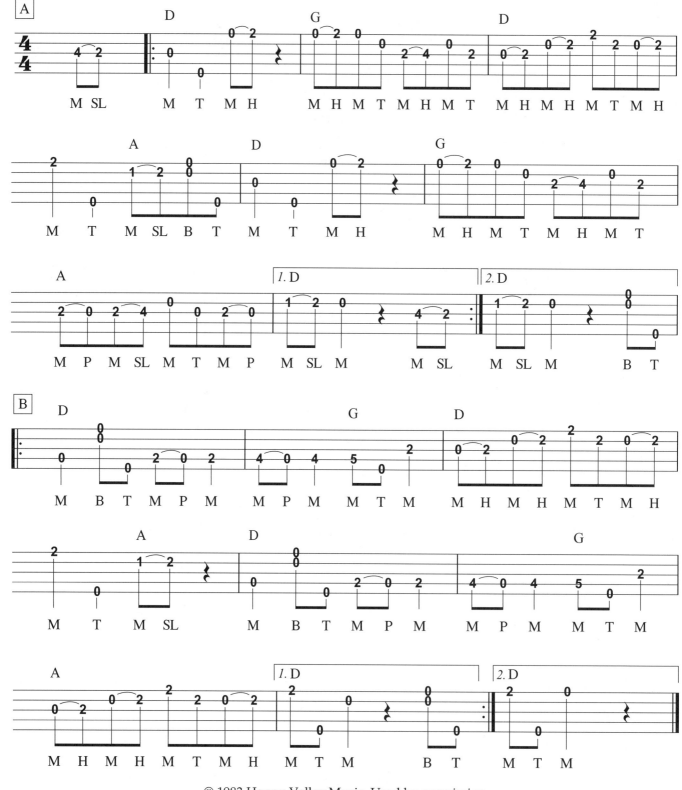

Sullivan's Hollow

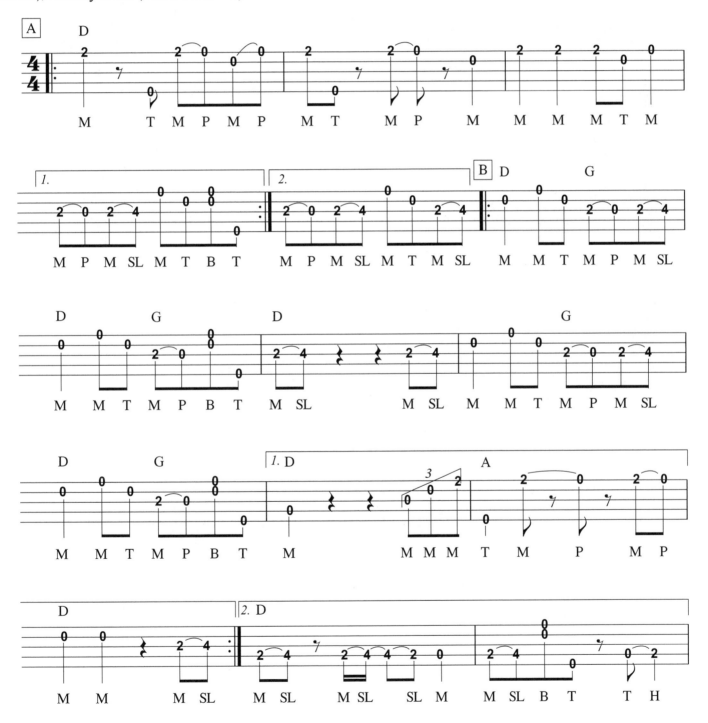 TRACK 27

Source: Carl Baron

0132-1/4b

GCGCD-Capo 2

"Sullivan's Hollow refers to an actual and evidently colorful spot near Lorena in Smith County (Mississippi), a part of the Bienville National Forest." Dave Freeman

Techniques: Galax lick: brush-see "Briar Picker Brown"; held note-see "Big Scioty".

Recordings: **Traditional Fiddle Music of Mississippi-Volume Two,** Freeny's Barn Dance Band (Country Records); **Kenny Hall** (Philo Records)

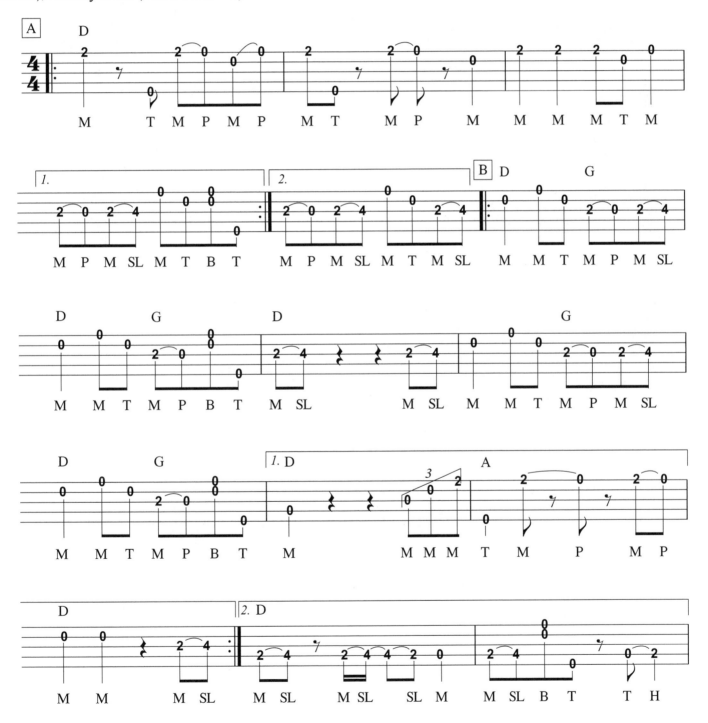

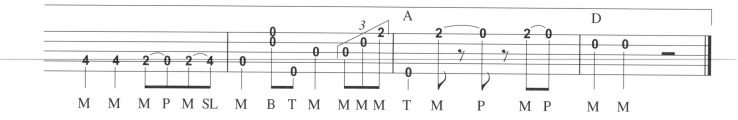

Cheick Hamala Diabate, master Malian musician and Bob Carlin at the time of their Grammy nominated CD <u>From Mali to America.</u> Photograph by Sam Radziviliuk

Tempy

TRACK 28

Source: Plank Road String Band and Tommy Jarrell

0132-1/2a

GCGCD-Capo 2

"Tempy" is a version of "I Wish I Was A Mole in the Ground".
Techniques: Held note –see "Big Scioty"; brush pull off –see "Box the Fox"
Recordings: Tommy Jarrell's Banjo Album (County Records); **Plank Road String Band** (June Appal Records)

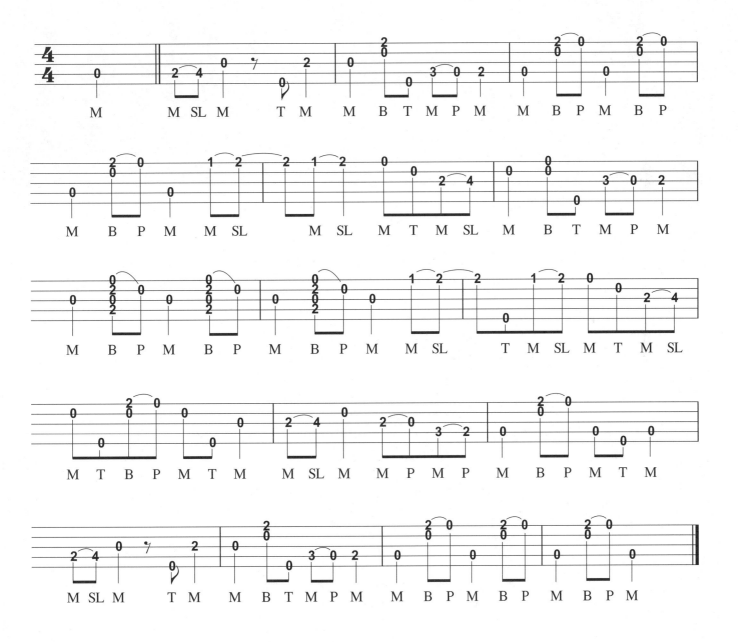

Bob and Tommy Jarrel playing music in Tommy's living room, circa 1978.
Photographer unknown.

Tempy roll down your bangs (2x)
Roll down your bangs and see how they hang
Tempy roll down your bangs.

My baby wants a five dollar shawl (2x)
So when I come round the hill with that twenty dollar bill
She says daddy where you been so long?

My baby where you been so long (2x)
I've been in the pen with those rough and rowdy men
And darling I'm going back again.

I wish I was a mole in that ground (2x)
If I was a mole in the ground, I'd root this mountain down
I wish I was a mole in that ground.

I wish I was a lizard in that spring (2x)
If I was a lizard in the spring I'd hear my darling sing
I wish I was a lizard in that spring

Tempy let your bangs hang down (2x)
Let your bangs hand down and roll them all around
Tempy let your bangs hang down.

Tippy, Get Your Haircut

TRACK 29

Source: Melvin Wine

0172-1/6   FBbFCD

"Melvin's father learned this tune from a neighbor, a black fiddler named Jilly Grace", -Alan Jabbour and Carl Fleischhauer. Melvin plays it in the key of G.

Tuning: See "Bob Carlin's Dream"
Techniques: Brush pull off – see "Box the Fox"; open string pull off – see "Bob Carlin's Dream"
Recordings: Cold Frost Morning, Melvin Wine (Poplar Records)

Bob Carlin in conversation with fiddler Melvin Wine (on left) at the Kent State Folk Festival, Kent, Ohio, date and photographer unknown.

Trouble

TRACK 30

Source: Stella and Taylor Kimble

0132-2/3

FDGCD-Capo 2

On my first trip down south, Ray Alden and Dave Spilkia took me to Meadows of Dan, Virginia, to visit the Kimbles. Both were in their eighties at that time and had been brought together by their renewed interest in the old-time music of their youth. After we played some tunes for the Kimble's (which, shades of role reversal, Taylor taped on his cassette machine to learn at a later time), they played us this tune and taught us the words that I sing here. Dave and Ray have since produced an album including the music of the Kimble's. This tune is in mountain minor tuning (GDGCD) with the fifth string dropped to an F.

Using the following chord position the tuning becomes the key of G.

Recordings: Eight Miles Apart, the Kimble's (Heritage Records);
It's All Gone Now, Ace Weems and the Fat Meat Boys (Carryon Records).

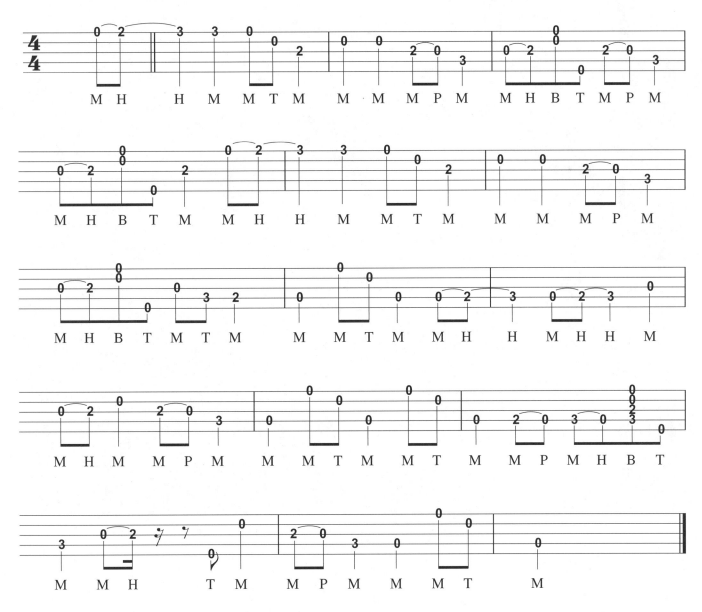

I never knew my troubles were so bad, they were so bad (2x)
The worse, the worse, worst I've ever had.

When your troubles get like mine, buddy, move on down that line
I never knew my trouble so bad, they were so bad
The worse, the worse, worst I've ever had.

My sugar baby's gone and she's left me in the wrong
I never knew my trouble were so bad, they were so bad
The worse, the worse, worst I've ever had

My sugar baby's dead and the very last words she said
Was never let that man get his way, get his way.

Bob Carlin with his custom Bart Reiter model banjo.
Photograph by Tom McNabb

Waiting for Nancy

TRACK 31

Source: Greg Canote

0172-2/1

GCGCD-Capo 2

On my first trip to California in 1980, I was introduced to Greg and Jere Canote by our mutual friend, Danny Gardella. The Canotes' aka The Small Wonder String Band aka the Spoonoplians perform at concerts and dances with Sandy Bradley. "Nancy" can be found in printed form in Curtis Bouterse's book of original tunes for the fretless banjo Nixon's Farewell.

Recordings: That Old Gut Feeling, Bertrum Levy (Flying Fish Records)

by Curtis Bouterse

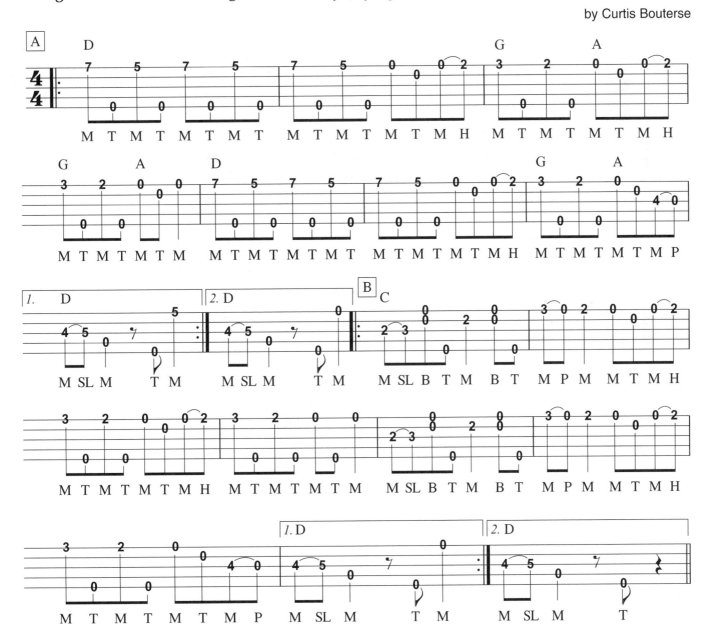

Alternate

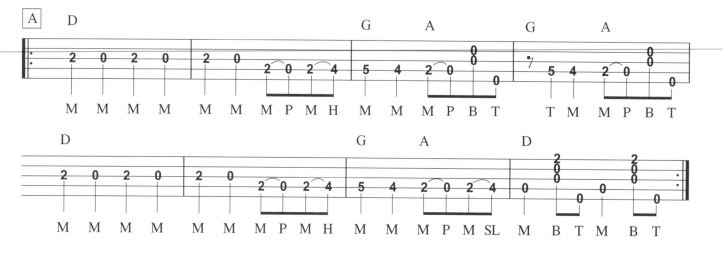

Bob Carlin (on the left with banjo) sits in with Dirk Powell/Fiddle and Tim O'Brien/Guitar at the 2000 Grey Fox Festival in New York State. Photograph by Frank Serio.

Where Did You Get That Hat

TRACK 32

Source: Mike Gallagher and the Corklickers

0172-1/2

GCGCD

This song, of music hall origins, was recorded in the 1920s by Gid Tanner and Fate Norris of Skillet Licker's fame for Columbia Records. My version is an amalgam of the words found in an 1888 printing of the song and a tune supplied by Philadelphia banjoist/fiddler Mike Gallagher.

Techniques: brush pull off – see "Box the Fox"; held note and brush hammer on-see "Big Scioty"

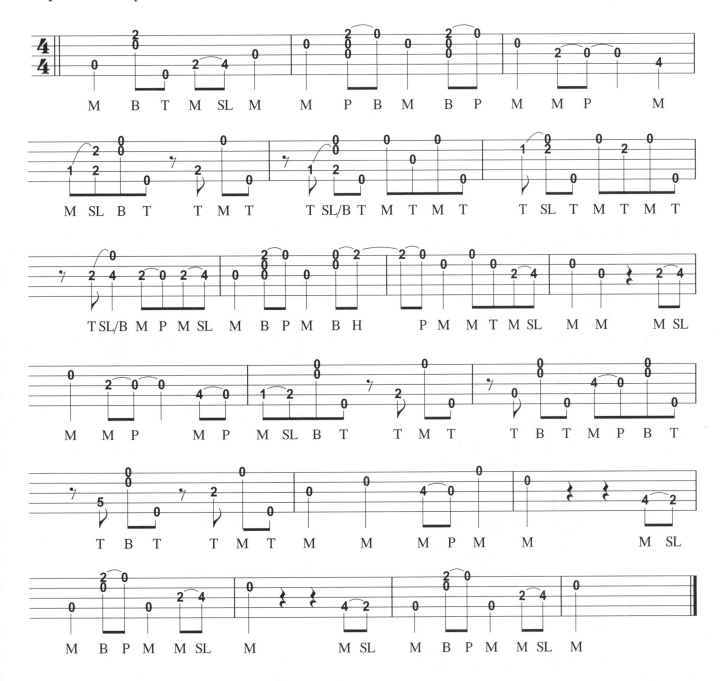

Well, how I came to get this hat it's very strange and funny
My grandfather died and left to me his property and money
And when the will was read out, they told me straight and flat
If I would have his money I must always were his hat.

Chorus:

Where Did You Get That Hat, where did you that tile
Isn't it a nobby one and just the proper style
I should like to have one, just the same as that
Where ever I go they shout hello where did you get that hat.

If I go to the opera house in that opera season
Someone is sure to shout at me without the slightest reason
If I go to a chowder club to have a jolly spree
There's someone in the party who is sure to shout at me

Chorus

At twenty-one I thought I would to my sweetheart get married
The people in the neighborhood had said too long we'd tarried
So off to the church we went right quick determined to get wed
I had not long been there when the parson to me said

Bob Carlin on stage with fiddler Joe Thompson, Pam Davis is on bass, and Clyde Davis on guitar. Guilford College, Greensboro, NC. Date and photographer unknown.

More Great Banjo Books from Centerstream...

Those using
Centerstream
Books & DVDs

The Competition